# Come on, horse
# and other stories

Hannie Truijens

Nelson

# Jip and Ben

Jip and Ben were going to a party.
They put on their big hats and
their small ties.
"You look good," said Ben.
"So do you," said Jip.

Jip and Ben walked down the road.
A big red truck came around the
bend too fast.
A big white bag fell off the truck.

The bag fell next to Jip and Ben and broke open.

"You are all white," said Jip.

"So are you," said Ben.

Jip and Ben walked down the road.
A big green truck came around the
bend too fast.
A big black bag fell off the truck.

The bag fell next to Jip and Ben and
broke open.

"You are all black," said Jip.

"So are you," said Ben.

Jip and Ben walked
over the bridge.
A big yellow truck went
over the bridge too fast.
Jip and Ben had to jump
into the river.

Jip and Ben came out
of the water.
"You are all wet," said Jip.
"So are you," said Ben.
"We must get dry."

Jip and Ben went to dry their big
hats and their small ties.
"I am dry now," said Jip.
"So am I," said Ben.
"Let's go to the party."

# Come on, horse

Sam went for a ride on his horse.

"Come on, horse," he said.

"I want to go fast."

"Neigh, neigh," said the horse.

"Hello, Jip," said Sam.

"Do you want a ride on my horse?"

"Yes, I do," said Jip.

"Get on the back," said Sam.

"Neigh, neigh," said the horse.

"Hello, Ben," said Sam.

"Do you want a ride on my horse?"

"Yes, I do," said Ben.

"Get on the front," said Sam.

"Neigh, neigh," said the horse.

"Hello, Meg," said Sam.

"Do you want a ride on my horse?"

"Yes, I do," said Meg.

"Get on his head," said Sam.

"Neigh, neigh," said the horse.

"Hello, Deb," said Sam.

"Do you want a ride on my horse?"

"Yes, I do," said Deb.

"Get on his tail," said Sam.

"Neigh, neigh," said the horse.

"Come on, horse," said Sam.
"We want to go faster.
Faster, FASTER, **FASTER**."
"Neigh, neigh," said the horse.

The horse stopped.

Up went Sam and Jip and Ben and Meg and Deb.

Down came Sam and Jip and Ben and Meg and Deb.

"Hee-hee," said the horse.

# As strong as you

Mr Hare walked up to
Mr Lion and said,
"You are very strong, but I
am as strong as you."
Mr Lion opened one eye.
"Show me," he said.

Mr Hare walked up to
Mrs Crocodile and said,
"You are very strong,
but I am as strong as you."
Mrs Crocodile opened one eye.
"Show me," she said.

Mr Hare tied a rope
to Mr Lion's tail.
"I will tie the other end to my
tail," he said.
"Wait until I tell you to pull."
Mr Lion closed his eyes.

Mr Hare ran to Mrs Crocodile and
tied the other end of the rope
to her tail.
"Wait until I tell you to pull,"
he said.
Mrs Crocodile closed her eyes.

"Now pull," shouted Mr Hare.
Mr Lion and Mrs Crocodile began
to pull.
They pulled and pulled but they
could not move at all.

Mr Lion and Mrs Crocodile pulled
all day long.
They got very cross.
"Do you give up?" said Mr Hare.
"Yes," they said.

Mr Lion and Mrs Crocodile stopped pulling.
Mr Hare untied Mr Lion's tail.
"I showed you, didn't I?" he said.
He then untied Mrs Crocodile's tail.
"I showed you, didn't I?" he said.

Mr Hare started to show off.
"I am as strong as a lion and
as strong as a crocodile," he said.
"And full of tricks," said Mr Owl
from his tree.